Settling the Frontier

ISBN-13: 978-0-15-358780-1
ISBN-10: 0-15-358780-6

3 4 5 6 7 8 9 10   179   11 10 09 08

Harcourt
SCHOOL PUBLISHERS

Visit *The Learning Site!* www.harcourtschool.com

Europeans in North America

READ TO FIND OUT **Why did Europeans come to North America?**

In 1492, Christopher Columbus left Spain to find a new route to Asia. He did not reach Asia. Columbus found North America. When he returned to Spain, he talked about a new land and the people who lived there. He brought back plants, animals, and gold. Soon, stories of this new land were told all over Europe.

Columbus hoped to reach Asia by crossing the Atlantic Ocean.

This is what preparing a meal would have looked like in colonial Jamestown.

Other countries sent people to North America. These people explored the land. They met Native Americans. They found new goods to trade. Spain, France, and England started colonies. A **colony** is an area ruled by a faraway government.

Many people came to live in North America. Some wanted to find gold. Some wanted to trade with Native Americans. Others wanted freedom of religion.

READING CHECK ⓧ CAUSE AND EFFECT **Why did Europeans come to North America?**

THE FRENCH AND INDIAN WAR

READ TO FIND OUT **How did the French and Indian War change the Ohio Valley?**

By the 1750s, both the French and the British controlled land in the Ohio Valley. Both groups wanted to control trade in the area.

Soon, fighting broke out. The French had many Native American groups as their allies. **Allies** are groups that help one another.

British General James Wolfe died in a battle during the French and Indian War.

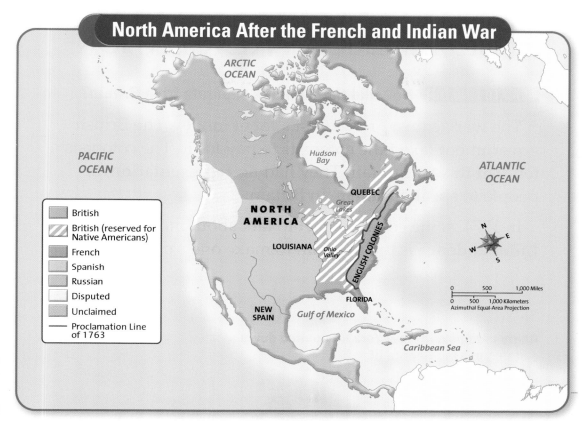

North America After the French and Indian War

British
British (reserved for Native Americans)
French
Spanish
Russian
Disputed
Unclaimed
Proclamation Line of 1763

ARCTIC OCEAN
PACIFIC OCEAN
Hudson Bay
ATLANTIC OCEAN
QUEBEC
Great Lakes
NORTH AMERICA
LOUISIANA
Ohio Valley
ENGLISH COLONIES
FLORIDA
NEW SPAIN
Gulf of Mexico
Caribbean Sea

0   500   1,000 Miles
0   500   1,000 Kilometers
Azimuthal Equal-Area Projection

France lost nearly all their lands in North America after the French and Indian War.

In 1763, the war was over. The British and the French signed a **treaty**. A treaty is an agreement between two nations. France had to give up its land in the Ohio Valley. British settlers soon began to move into the area.

The Native Americans who already lived there were unhappy. They attacked British settlers. The British king tried to stop the fighting. He said part of the lands belonged to the Native Americans.

READING CHECK ☼ **CAUSE AND EFFECT** **How did the French and Indian War change the Ohio Valley?**

THE AMERICAN REVOLUTION

READ TO FIND OUT **How did the colonies separate from Britain?**

The war against France cost a lot of money. The British government taxed the colonists to pay for it. The colonists felt that this was unfair. They had no **representation**, or people to speak for them, in Britain.

In 1774, some colonists met to talk about independence. **Independence** is the freedom to make one's own laws.

Angry colonists in New York City pulled down a statue of King George III.

Fort Laurens was the only American fort built in the Ohio Valley during the American Revolution.

Fighting between British soldiers and the colonists began in 1775. It was the start of the American Revolution. In Ohio, the British asked Native Americans to attack settlers. There were many fights between Native Americans and settlers.

The war ended in 1783. The Americans won. Britain had to give the Americans their freedom. They also had to give much of their land in North America to the Americans.

READING CHECK SUMMARIZE **How did the colonies separate from Britain?**

THE NORTHWEST TERRITORY

READ TO FIND OUT How did life change for settlers and Native Americans after the American Revolution?

After the war, the United States of America was a new country. It owed money to American soldiers, farmers, and merchants who had helped during the war.

Congress decided to repay these people by giving them land in the Northwest Territory. A **territory** is an area owned and governed by a country.

The Northwest Territory included lands that are now the states of Ohio, Michigan, Indiana, Illinois, Wisconsin, and part of Minnesota.

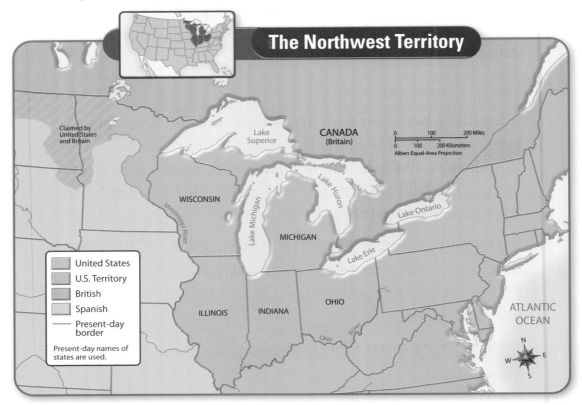

The Northwest Territory

Claimed by United States and Britain

Lake Superior

CANADA (Britain)

0   100   200 Miles
0   100   200 Kilometers
Albers Equal-Area Projection

WISCONSIN

Lake Huron

Lake Michigan

Lake Ontario

Mississippi River

MICHIGAN

Lake Erie

United States
U.S. Territory
British
Spanish
Present-day border
Present-day names of states are used.

ILLINOIS   INDIANA   OHIO

Ohio River

ATLANTIC OCEAN

N
W   E
S

The Northwest Territory was divided into townships by surveyors.

In 1787, Congress passed the Northwest Ordinance. An **ordinance** is a law. This law told how the Northwest Territory would be governed. It said how a part of the territory could become a state. It also promised settlers freedom of religion.

Native Americans were already living there. They did not want to lose their lands.

READING CHECK ŏ **CAUSE AND EFFECT** How did life change for settlers and Native Americans after the American Revolution?

Surveyor Tools

Background Surveyors needed special tools to mark areas of land in the Ohio Valley. These tools were used to measure and mark the boundaries of the land.

SURVEY CHAIN

Surveyors stretched out chains to measure land.

SURVEY PLAT

Maps like this one were made by surveyors of the Northwest Territory.

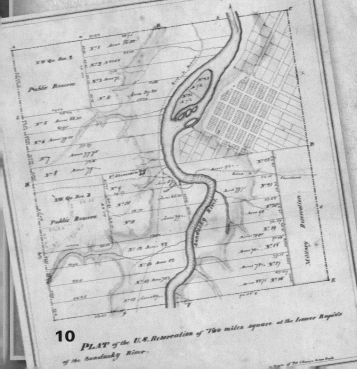

PLAT of the U.S. Reservation of Two miles square at the Lower Rapids of the Sandusky River.

COMPASS

A compass helped the surveyor know in which direction he was looking.

TRIPOD AND JACOB'S STAFF

These bases held other tools, like a telescope.

TELESCOPE

A telescope was placed on top of a base. A surveyor would look through the telescope to line up the boundary lines.

1 Why did surveyors need survey chains?

2 When would a Jacob's staff be most useful to a surveyor?

THE FRONTIER WARS

READ TO FIND OUT How did the frontier wars change life for Native Americans?

In the 1790s, Native Americans in the Northwest Territory wanted settlers to leave Native American lands. Many Native Americans decided to **unite**, or join, to fight the settlers.

Native Americans and American soldiers fought many battles. Some Native Americans wanted peace, but others continued to fight.

THE FRONTIER WARS

Native Americans led by Michikinikwa defeat American forces led by Arthur St. Clair

The Battle of Fallen Timbers is fought

1791

In 1794, American soldiers fought Native Americans at the Battle of Fallen Timbers. The Native Americans lost. In 1795, Native American and American leaders signed a peace treaty.

Native Americans later had to give most of the land in Ohio to the Americans. They kept only a small area of land in Ohio. Some of them had to leave Ohio.

READING CHECK ⚙ **CAUSE AND EFFECT How did the frontier wars change life for Native Americans?**

American forces led by General Anthony Wayne win the Battle of Fallen Timbers

The Treaty of Greenville is signed

1794

1795

Activity 1

Use each word in a sentence to explain its meaning.

1. territory _____
   _____

2. ordinance _____
   _____

3. allies _____
   _____

4. representation _____
   _____

5. unite _____
   _____

6. colony _____
   _____

7. treaty _____
   _____

8. independence _____
   _____

Activity 2

Look at the list of vocabulary words. Categorize the vocabulary words in a chart like the one below. Then use a glossary or dictionary to learn the definitions of the words that sound familiar or that you do not know.

conquistador	colony	slavery
mission	missionary	profit
allies	alliance	treaty
frontier	rebellion	proclamation
tax	representation	Parliament
independence	congress	militia
revolution	debt	territory
ordinance	township	right
unite		

		I Know	Sounds Familiar	Don't Know
○	militia			✓
	revolution		✓	
	colony	✓		

(Focus Skill) **Cause and Effect** What were some effects that European settlement of North America had on Native Americans?

Vocabulary

1. How are the terms **territory** and **ordinance** related?

Recall

2. Why did the British government tax the colonists?
3. How did the American government pay people who had helped during the American Revolution?
4. Why did Native Americans attack settlers after the American Revolution?

Critical Thinking

5. Why did the French and the British start fighting in the 1750s?

Activity

Make a Time Line On a separate sheet of paper, make a time line of events in North America. The time line should begin at 1492 and end at 1795.

Photo credits Front Cover North Wind Picture Archives/Alamy; 2 Bridgeman Art Library, New York, NY; 3 Richard T. Nowitz/Corbis; 4 Bridgeman Art Library, New York, NY; 10 (bl) Bettman/Corbis; (tr) Rutherford B. Hayes Presidential Center; 11 (tr) National Museum of American History, Smithsonian Institution/Greensdale Collection; (c) National Museum of American History, Smithsonian Institution/ Greensdale Collection; (br) Bridgeman Art Library, New York, NY; 13 (br) Bridgeman Art Library, New York, NY